On the Professional Code of Ethics and Business Conduct in the Workplace

Professional Ethics: 100 Tips to Improve Your Professional Life

Richard G Lowe, Jr

On the Professional Code of Ethics and Business Conduct in the Workplace

Professional Ethics: 100 Tips to Improve Your Professional Life

Business Professional Series #1

Published by The Writing King
www.thewritingking.com

On the Professional Code of Ethics and Business Conduct in the Workplace

ASIN: B016SFKTJC
ISBN: 978-1-943517-77-0 (Hardcover)
ISBN: 978-1-943517-76-3 (Paperback)
ISBN: 978-1-943517-13-8 (eBook)

Audiobook narrated by Melissa J. Costa.

Table of Contents

Table of Contents

Introduction

"The difference between an amateur and a professional is in their habits. An amateur has amateur habits. A professional has professional habits. We can never free ourselves from habit. But we can replace bad habits with good ones." —
Steven Pressfield

Success on the job can be a mystery; sometimes it appears that there's no way to get ahead except for random chance or familial connections, or, worse yet, brown-nosing the boss. It is annoying to know and to see someone who doesn't deserve a promotion move up the ladder quickly while you are lucky if you get standard cost-of-living raises.

"I think it's important to always keep professional and surround yourself with good people, work hard, and be nice to everyone." —Caroline Winberg

On the other side of the fence, being the boss might seem like heaven on earth, but it's really not all that it's cracked up to be. Believe it or not, most people who hold the position of boss, or even such esteemed titles as CEO, CFO, or COO, have just as many or even more insecurities and problems as you.

In fact, because the boss handles more than just himself, his problems are magnified by all of the people on the team, plus the people on adjoining teams.

During my long career in the computer industry and as the Director of Computer Operations at Trader Joe's, I've been on

Introduction

both sides of the fence. I think the most critical fact is there isn't a rulebook. There are few, if any, classes in school that teach you how to be a good employee or boss.

Of course, there are courses on how to do aspects of the job, such as how to program, how to fill in a balance sheet, or how to create a Gantt chart. There are also excellent courses on how to manage projects, how to investigate problems, and even how to supervise people.

But there really isn't a book or class that tells you how to act in the workplace, regardless of whether you are the supervised or supervisor. It's kind of like being married and raising a family. There are lots of classes, books, and courses, but nothing can prepare you for the actual reality.

I found during my 35 years in the workplace that the things that always tripped me up had nothing to do with the technology or the information that I was working with. Technology and information can always be handled with learning, classes, or even consultants.

The problem comes from patterns of behavior that are destructive, or at the very least don't help. For example, sarcasm is one of these behavioral quirks that many people think is funny and useful. While arguably there may be some value in sarcasm, it has no valid place in the office at all.

Email etiquette is another one of those things that trip up people in the workplace all the time. Someone might think a slightly off-color joke is funny and send it out to everyone in the office. That's always a mistake—sometimes a career-ending one.

Another person might think it's okay to hang a risqué poster on the wall next to his desk—say in a fire department, for example—and in these modern times, that's not acceptable either.

Meetings are another area that are so poorly handled in American business that sometimes it's amazing that any work it's done at all. Your typical meeting in virtually all workplace settings consists of an unorganized mob with no agenda, little control, no record of what happened, and the appropriate people may not even be invited.

Having a job and doing work is often paramount, but it shouldn't take precedence over everything else. Yes, a job does pay the bills, and it enables one to support a family and perhaps have some fun now and then, but you should work for your life, not live for your job. It's a matter of setting priorities, and it's amazing how many of us set them incorrectly and wind up unhappy and ill.

I decided to write this book to help fill that gap of knowledge about what is appropriate and acceptable in the workplace, for both the boss and the subordinate. Additionally, many behaviors are unacceptable in the workplace, and this book goes over some of those.

This is a short book and thus is an overview of what I view as professional ethics. It describes a way for professionals to behave ethically in the workplace, and as regards work.

There are many examples, and all are from real-life, but the names have been changed to protect the innocent and the

Introduction

guilty alike. Sometimes the details have been modified slightly to preserve the privacy of the people involved.

I hope you enjoy what I've written and find it to be of some value. If you would like to send me a note about this book, feel free to write me at rich@thewritingking.com. If you enjoyed the book, please write a positive review.

Teammates

"The important thing is that your teammates have to know you're pulling for them and you really want them to be successful." —Kobe Bryant

Regardless of whether you are the boss, the subordinate, or just an intern hanging out for a week, there are almost always other people working with and around you. These are teammates. Sometimes they are employees, sometimes consultants, and occasionally service personnel brought in for specific tasks.

It is important—vital—to treat everyone in the workplace, regardless of rank, with respect. If you're the owner of a mom-and-pop business in a strip mall or the CEO of a multibillion-dollar, multinational firm, you should still treat the lowliest janitor or intern with the same amount of respect that you would give to the president of your largest territory.

It works the other way as well. Wherever you are in the organization, you depend on the people who are around you. The receptionist is important, as she routes communications, the janitor keeps the area clean, computer programmers create the software that runs the business, and delivery people bring packages to your desk.

You might believe that you are the hottest up-and-coming star in the world, and that may actually be true, but you still depend on the people around you. Presumably, in one way or another, the people around you depend on you as well.

Teammates

Every person in the environment observes your behavior and makes conclusions based on what they see. On that day when you were in a foul mood and treated the receptionist poorly, yelling at her and calling her a worthless bimbo, someone in the office saw what you did and everyone heard about it before very long. All of those people formed a negative opinion of you because of your actions.

Treat each person in the workplace with respect; that means everyone regardless of their status, their position in the company, or whether or not they can do something for you.

Respect

Respect is earned. When you first start working, no one knows who you are or what you can do. They may have read your resume, or looked online and found your LinkedIn profile or learned about you from other people. However, until they meet you and see you in action, they don't really know you, your capabilities, or your personality.

Generally, you are given the benefit of the doubt when you start at a new workplace. No one knows who you are or what you can do, but you usually have some time to make a good impression.

The respect you will be granted as time goes on depends upon your actions, how will you perform, how will you treat others, and your personal ethics. If you are a high performer who tends to get things done, you may get a lot of respect. If, on the other hand, you treat people poorly, that will drop.

Why is respect important? If I respect someone, I will go the extra mile for them not only to get things done but to get them done right. Someone who's respected can cause others to want to meet the goal, to desire to work for the company, and to do what's needed to get the job done.

On the other hand, someone who is not respected may find it difficult to get volunteers for a particular project, or to get that vital program done ahead of schedule. Sometimes the fear of losing a job can take the place of respect, but it doesn't go very far.

How do you get respect?

> ➢ Be on your best behavior
> ➢ Be honest with others
> ➢ Understand the needs and wants of others
> ➢ Maintain your integrity
> ➢ Be productive and competent
> ➢ Don't talk about others behind their back
> ➢ Be willing to stand up for yourself and others
> ➢ Don't demand that others do things that you wouldn't be willing to do yourself

This doesn't mean that you should allow yourself to get walked on by others, used, or abused. People who roll over when they are harmed or threatened are never respected.

HONESTY

In the workplace, honesty is vital to personal survival. The dishonest person may appear to be doing well, but they never last for very long.

Teammates

Of course, that doesn't mean you should everyone every little detail about everything. Just be truthful, regardless if it hurts. If you screwed up, be willing to admit it and do what's needed to make up any damage that you did.

PERSONAL LIVES

It's always tempting to talk to others in the workplace about your life outside work. I know, I've done it; we all have. Through long experience, though, I found it best to keep my "real" life far away from the workplace.

No one at your job wants to hear about your divorce, the problems you're having with your wife at home, or that your child is using drugs in high school. That's not the proper venue to discuss such things.

If you take the attitude that the workplace is for work and that anything is not work has no place in the office, then you'll do well.

This applies not only to talk but to actions. The boss who takes long lunches for personal reasons, or the employee who's always ducking out to run some errands are engaged in inappropriate behavior in the workplace.

ROMANCE AT WORK

As a general rule, and there are exceptions, it is always best to refrain from any kind of romantic or sexual involvement in the office.

Obviously people who are dating or married that work in the same office will be affectionate with each other, but they should keep in mind that the workplace is for work and not for romance.

Making any kind of sexual comment in the office, regardless of your status toward the other person, is completely out of line and inappropriate. Unless you're working on a porn set, sex has no place on the job. There are no exceptions to this rule.

One of the issues in the workplace for many people is their social life. I know when I was younger and working, most of the people that I ran into on a regular basis where those I worked with in the office. I began to feel an affinity for some of the employees, including several women. This is only normal; when people work closely together, they start to feel an affinity toward one another.

Regardless, tread very cautiously while pursuing a romantic or sexual relationship with another person in the same office. These affairs may work out, but by far most of the time the only outcome is trouble.

The HR director used to take great delight in telling stories at our yearly sexual-harassment seminar about some of the things that went on throughout the corporation. In my mind, the behavior described was truly horrifying and abhorrent to anyone with any kind of ethics or integrity.

There are plenty of people to date outside of the office, and numerous places to meet others who might be of interest. You would be wise to keep your romantic or sexual liaisons away from the workplace. This is not just because they can lead to trouble in the human resources department, but because they

Teammates

can reduce the respect that others have for you and make it harder for you to get your job done.

Summary

> ➢ Earn respect via your actions towards others
> ➢ Be honest, even if you have to admit a mistake
> ➢ Keep your personal life at home
> ➢ Treat all your teammates with respect
> ➢ Don't engage in office romance
> ➢ Anything sexual is not appropriate in the workplace

Leadership and Responsibility

"If your actions inspire others to dream more, learn more, do more and become more, you are a leader." —John Quincy Adams

"A leader is one who knows the way, goes the way, and shows the way." —John C. Maxwell

Leadership is the ability to cause others to move in a desirable direction. It really is that simple. Using this definition, Adolf Hitler would not be considered as a leader, as the direction that he moved Germany was not desirable by any sane definition and led to its destruction in a very bloody war.

Thus, the ability to move people in a direction is not what makes a leader. It is the capacity to move them in a direction that is constructive and fulfill the goals of the organization.

A good leader

> ➢ Sets achievable goals for the organization
> ➢ Leads others to achieve those goals
> ➢ Takes full responsibility for the organization
> ➢ Creates an environment where those in the organization thrive
> ➢ Understands and appreciates the needs and desires of his teammates

Over the years, I have worked for many different people who accepted the role as *the boss*. Some of these people were my

Leadership and Responsibility

direct supervisor. Some had the title of CEO, president, COO, vice president, and other fancy words.

Something that I've learned from hard experience is that the title means nothing, absolutely nothing at all. Just because a person says he is a CEO does not mean that person is competent, a leader, takes responsibility, or provides any value to the organization.

For example, there was a time where I worked directly for the CEO of a corporation, and I remember it is one of the most fulfilling and valuable moments of my entire career. He was extraordinarily well-respected by everyone in the corporation, and as I worked for him, I learned the reasons behind that respect.

He had a unique ability to say just a few words and make a person feel like he'd been heard and understood. He would take the time to explain, in very few words, what needed to be done, in a way that granted responsibility and power.

I put together a proposal for a new application system for our accounting department. It wasn't going to be cheap, and I was very hesitant to present it to him because it was the first time I had to deal with him directly. I made sure I did a good job to justify why we needed to outlay the expense.

When I approached him with the proposal in hand, he told me not to worry about the finance. He explained that finance was his job, adding that determining the correct technical solution was my mission, and he trusted me to do the right thing.

That same scenario occurred many times during the year that I worked for him. Even on the occasions where he declined my proposals, I felt like that at least I'd been heard, understood, and that his concerns were valid.

My respect for this man was so great that if he'd asked me to go to battle for him I would have happily led the charge. In my mind, that's leadership. Because of the immense respect that I held for him, I was never going to let him or the company down and went out of my way to ensure the highest quality for the best solution possible.

Bad Apples

Every team I've ever been on has had a bad apple or two. By that, I mean the team member who isn't even trying, who has severe problems getting the job done, or who creates conflicts within the workplace.

As a manager, you should always remember that honest and productive people deserve your attention and help. When you find someone who isn't doing his or her job properly, the first thing to do is to investigate and find out if there's something that you can do to help. Does the person need additional training? Do they need classes in assertiveness or anger management? In other words, is there something that you, the manager, can do to correct the situation with the person?

At my first job, the bad apple was a woman who got drunk at lunch every single day. She more-or-less ceased to be productive in the afternoons. She was a bad apple and should've been fired. Eventually she quit, which made it easier for everyone.

At another job, we had a technical person who was demonstrably grossly incompetent. He was simply not doing his job at all, and this was proven by an independent investigation by external contractors. He was fired with cause, but it took entirely too long and he caused a lot of damage before he left.

A bad apple can also be a person who is unduly negative or unsupportive of other team members. I've worked with team members who snarled at others regularly, growled at clients,

Bad Apples

cursed in the office, and generally made themselves unpleasant.

As a manager and a leader, you should expect—no, you should demand—that everyone under your authority acts competently and professionally. This is only fair to each person in the group, as a bad apple interferes with and lets down everyone.

As a team member, regardless of your position in the company, you should be willing to accept responsibility for the whole group. This means if someone on the team is not living up to high standards of professionalism and competence, you should take steps to deal with it. This could mean offering your help, becoming a mentor, or even reporting the person to your boss or supervisor.

If you tolerate unprofessional behavior or incompetence, then you have no right to complain.

"The professionalism and competence level in the workplace falls to the level of tolerance. You want a fun, happy place to work? Don't tolerate bad apples." —Richard Lowe

One of the most frustrating experiences that I've had is not being allowed to fire someone who was incompetent, malicious, or unproductive. This is often because the human resources department tends to believe their job is to protect the company or corporation from legal action.

I found that the fact that is missed is the damage caused by an incompetent or malicious employee far outweighs, in most cases, the cost of lawsuits. A bad apple affects the morale of everyone around them, causes quality problems in whatever is being produced, upsets customers, and can even lead to disaster.

A manager needs to work quickly to address and handle unprofessional, incompetent, or unethical behavior by any team member under their responsibility. This could mean anything from setting up a program to correcting the behavior or terminating the employee if the situation does not improve.

The bad apple must be handled quickly. The rot from allowing someone to continue unproductive and malicious behavior only grows greater as time passes and it can become difficult, if not impossible, to correct.

One of the major issues with tolerating bad apples is they can successfully fight termination by claiming their work was sufficient in the past, so why are they being "picked on" now? Prevent this defense by jumping on issues immediately instead of letting them fester.

Summary

> ➤ A good leader treats others with respect
> ➤ To be a good leader you have to listen, understand, and act with compassion
> ➤ Leaders lead, they don't follow
> ➤ Don't tolerate bad apples, take steps to get them productive to get them out of the workplace
> ➤ Do not manage using fear
> ➤ Create an environment where everybody in the workplace thrives

Bad Apples

Meetings

"The least productive people are usually the ones who are most in favor of holding meetings." —Thomas Sowell

Out of everything that happens in business, meetings waste more time than anything else. However, any meetings are necessary, as it is important to get team members on the same page, get input and advice, or hear and understand other viewpoints.

A well-managed meeting is an engaging experience for everyone involved. The correct people are invited, an agenda is created so people know how to prepare, and the meeting itself is short, quick, and to the point. Unfortunately, this kind of get-together is relatively rare in most businesses.

Most managers and supervisors simply don't know how to run a meeting. First of all, your average company typically schedules too many meetings. Presumably, the people in a job are there to get work done, not talk about it with everyone else.

Worse yet, meetings tend to go on much longer than necessary, start late, and waste time because the people who attend have not prepared or were not briefed in advance (by using an agenda) on the subject at hand.

Let's take an average meeting as an example. A supervisor decides he wants to get a group of people together to discuss project status. He invites his entire department of 12 people

Meetings

plus half a dozen from other groups. That's a total of 18 people coming to the meeting.

He schedules the meeting right after lunch and sets it for an hour long. Our average supervisor doesn't bother sending out an agenda so that people know what is expected to occur at the meeting. Two of the team members arrive 15 minutes late, so the meeting start time is delayed to wait for them. Another 15 minutes is spent briefing everyone on why they are there and what happened at the last meeting.

Thus, we are already 30 minutes into the scheduled time of the meeting and nothing useful has been discussed. Things finally get rolling and people are talking to each other. Of course, it's just after lunch so some will be a little lethargic from their meals. The meeting runs over by 45 minutes, and no one bothers to take minutes or detailed notes.

During my career, that was pretty much par for the course for any meeting, regardless of whether it was at the company I was working at, a client, or vendor. They virtually always ran the same.

Running a meeting in such a manner is unprofessional.

Let's start from the top. It is very rare that a well-run meeting requires more than half a dozen people, much less 18 as in the above example. Only those people who are part of the decision-making process or who need to be briefed should be invited. More is not better and tends to waste everyone's time.

There are exceptions, of course. Status meetings, or those called in an emergency, may require more attendees. However, still only invite those who need to be there.

An agenda should always be sent out in advance. In general, this should be a short list of decisions that need to be made, and topics that are going to be discussed. It is a list of "what" is to be discussed. There is no why, how, who, and other information—only what is to be decided and what is to be discussed. You should be able to create an agenda for your meeting in five to ten minutes. If you take much longer than that, you're making it too complicated.

Meetings should start on time. People who are late are disrespecting the time of everyone who was there. Being late to a meeting is unprofessional behavior, unless, of course, there is a good reason. Regardless of the reason or who is late, the meeting should start on time.

Assuming you are creating an agenda and minutes for each meeting, there generally is no need to go over what happened in the previous meeting. That just wastes everyone's time. Anything that was not resolved last time should have been added to the agenda of the current meeting.

Start the meeting with the first item on the agenda, which should be the highest priority item. Work down to the last item on the list, which should be the lowest priority item. As a general rule, if it's not on the agenda it doesn't get discussed. Alternately, new topics that come up in the meeting could be added to the end, or could be scheduled for a future meeting.

Meetings

Don't schedule your meetings for 30, 60, or 90 minutes. Instead, schedule them for 25, 50, or 75 minutes. I found this tends to make them run a little bit faster and more efficiently. It also gives time for someone to get to something else scheduled at the top of the next hour.

Try not to schedule breaks in the middle of your meetings. Quite often, a 10-minute break will extend to 30-minutes as you try and herd everyone back into the room. If your meeting is so long that it requires breaks, then you may actually want to create multiple sessions throughout the day.

Finish on time. If your meeting is scheduled to run from 10:00 AM to 10:50 AM, end at 10:50 AM. That's the reason why the agenda should be in the order of highest priority to lowest priority. If you run out of time, you at least make sure the highest priority items are addressed.

Making a hard and fast rule that meetings will finish on time tends to result in more productive discussions.

Meetings need to be managed tightly. A meeting takes up a large number of peoples' time. So run it tight, keep it to the point, and don't let people wander off-topic.

Everybody should be attentive. If you are running a meeting, ensure that there is no texting, stepping out to take phone calls and playing on laptops or tablets while the meeting is going on.

Make it a firm rule that except for note taking, there should be absolutely no use of computers in the meeting.

One of my team members had a habit of using his smart phone to send texts during meetings. In the course of an hour, he would send and receive a couple of dozen messages. Partially as a result—and also due to low engagement—he did not contribute anything of any consequence to any meeting that he ever attended. His mind simply wasn't there.

Everyone in attendance should be taking notes. Some people use a tablet, some a computer, and some even a piece of paper. It doesn't matter. In fact, it is not important if they never look at the notes again. The process of taking the notes tends to help people remember the important points.

I have found that those who attend without taking notes tend to be poor contributors, and usually others don't receive any value from their attendance.

As soon as you can after the meeting is over, write up the minutes and send them out. Minutes should only record decisions that were made and what was discussed. Keep them short and to the point—anything over about half a page is not going to be read. If you've taken good notes, writing up minutes should require five or ten minutes at the most; if it takes longer, you're writing too much.

If you get in the habit of controlling your meetings in this matter, I think you'll find that they run quicker, more efficiently, and you get more done. On top of that, your day will become more productive because you're not wasting your time and the time of all your team members.

If you're attending a meeting, you can gently cause some of these practices to be put in place. When you get an invitation

Meetings

to a meeting, politely ask for the agenda. When the meeting is over, ask for the minutes. In other words, you can assert control so that you can better manage your time in meetings.

Summary

- Limit your invitations to those who can contribute to the meeting
- Create an agenda and distribute it well before the meeting so the attendees have a chance to read it
- Start your meeting on time; don't wait for latecomers
- Don't schedule meetings immediately after lunch if possible
- Schedule your meetings for a little bit less than the full half hour or hour
- Control the meeting and don't allow off-topic discussions
- Make sure everyone is paying attention
- Everyone at a meeting should be taking notes
- Ask people to turn off their cell phones or leave them outside the room
- End the meeting on time
- Send out minutes as soon after the meeting as you can

Email and Texting

"For email, the old postcard rule applies. Nobody else is supposed to read your postcards, but you'd be a fool if you wrote anything private on one." —Judith Martin

Throughout most of my career, I've longed for the days before email. Yes, I remember when there was no email. We actually had to use the phone on our desk, write things down on a piece of paper, or walk over to someone to deliver a message.

Email is an incredibly useful communication tool. Email is also one of the biggest time wasters ever been invented.

Both of these statements are equally true. Email is a great way to communicate. It's very reliable, very fast, and messages can be sorted and stored in folders so they can be looked at later.

On the other hand, much time is wasted throughout the day reading and rereading emails, reviewing and deleting spam, and trying to create the perfect message.

KEEP YOUR EMAILS SUCCINCT AND TO THE POINT

When composing your email message, keep it brief. People in the workforce are busy, and in most cases they'll only read the first paragraph anyway.

Ensure your email subject states what it is about. If your subject is poorly composed, then email may never be opened, much less read, at all.

Email and Texting

One of the people I supervised wrote incredibly long emails describing every single small detail of whatever he was writing about. It was not uncommon for a printed version of one message to go on for a dozen or more pages. He was very thorough and conscientious; unfortunately, others in the office mentioned they never even opened his messages because they were simply too long to confront.

The most vital information should be within the top two or three paragraphs of your message, and keep the total length to under a half page, printed out, if possible. In general, if your email is longer than that, it's too long.

Of course there are exceptions, and by all means if you need to write a longer message, do so.

Always spell check email messages, and reread it at least once to ensure the grammar is tolerable (at the least) and that it says what you really wanted to say.

EMAILS DO NOT COMMUNICATE EMOTION

When you're talking to somebody in person, you receive information on a variety of senses. You hear the tone of their voice; you can smell them and come to certain conclusions from that. You can see their reaction or emotions playing on their face. You can view their body language.

Absolutely none of that information is communicated in an email. An email generally contains strings of text, and occasionally a photo or video.

Human beings have a tendency to read emotion in that text, even when not as intended. For example, when my boss replied to an email with "yes," I invariably read more into that response than he intended. I'd wonder, for example, if my boss was angry or annoyed. Sometimes I would even act on those beliefs because of the curtness of his reply.

On many occasions I had to intervene after one of my subordinates sent a normal-seeming email which was interpreted as flippant or sarcastic. Over time, I became fascinated by the dynamics of communications via email and the problems that poorly thought out messages could unintentionally cause.

Spend a couple of extra seconds or minutes when you write an email to include a thank you or some other politeness to soften the tone of the message. That extra 30 seconds can save quite a bit of time on the backend having to defend yourself after the fact.

And, oh yes, don't use exclamation points and don't write in capital letters. These are both considered rude.

BE CAREFUL WITH HUMOR IN AN EMAIL

I had a gentleman working for me years ago who loved to include humor in all of his email messages. He would send out off-color jokes on a regular basis to other employees throughout the office. Unfortunately, this created a problem for some team members, because they didn't see the humor. It took a couple of verbal warnings, and finally a written warning, to get him to stop. I'm not sure he ever understood why it was inappropriate, but at least he stopped doing it.

Email and Texting

The problem with sending out of any kind of humor in email messages in office is that somebody is going to misinterpret that humor. This is not necessarily because they are sensitive or can't take a joke; frequently, there are people of other cultures, religions, and backgrounds honestly don't view what was said as humor. In fact, the humor could actually be offensive.

It's one thing to tell a group of people an off-color joke in person. It's an entirely different thing to send it in an email. The message can be forwarded, copied, and sent all over the entire office within a short period of time. It will get backed up and may survive in inboxes for years, and may wind up on on the desk of someone in Human Resources.

You can also look at it this way. When you tell a joke, there is no record (unless it's recorded) so you might be given the benefit of the doubt as to how it was received. In the case of an email message, the evidence is right there in black and white, and it becomes harder to defend yourself.

Don't use humor in email messages in a business environment.

ASSUME ALL EMAILS ARE READ BY HUMAN RESOURCES
All companies can read and review any employee email message at any point in time. They don't have to give notice, they don't have to mention it, and they don't need to justify it.

Some companies, in fact, have implemented automated scanning technologies to look for patterns which indicate harassment. Email messages containing certain phrases and keywords can be automatically forwarded to the human resources department for further review.

Your safest bet when sending an email from the office is to assume that it will wind up on the desk of the human resources office.

Compose all emails sent using corporate email accounts with those facts in mind. Since your message can wind up on anyone's desk, make sure that what you're writing doesn't violate company policy or cause a harassment issue.

DON'T USE CORPORATE EMAIL OR PHONES FOR PERSONAL PURPOSES

As tempting as it is, you should never use your corporate email (that's email provided to you by your job) for personal use. If your office gives you the phone or laptop, you should avoid using it for personal use, regardless of the company policy.

Company equipment belongs to the employer. It doesn't belong to you, and you have absolutely no rights over their administration and policing of their own property.

What this means is if you send emails of a personal nature using your corporate email account, don't be surprised if work reviews those emails. That's going to happen, and your office has every legal right to do whatever they want with emails that exist on their own server.

The company can also examine text messages that you send or receive on a company cell phone at will and without a warrant or even a reason. They don't need a warrant because the phone belongs to them, not you. The implication of this is if the police asks your boss for the text messages on your business phone, he can agree and, in that case, no warrant is required and no notification need be given to you.

The same is true of the email system. The emails that are on a corporate email server belong to the corporation, not you. So if you're sending explicit messages about your hot love affair using the corporate email system, then you shouldn't be shocked if the human resources department has a chat with you.

There was a time when my wife was very sick and was in the hospital. I made quite a few calls to the doctors and medical professionals about the matter using the company phone. The company didn't have any problem with this; in fact they gave me permission. After noticing that every call was listed on the corporate phone bill, I decided it was time to stop using the company phone for personal use.

Be a professional. Don't use company equipment, company email, and company phones for personal use. Otherwise, you might be allowing your job to gain access to information about you and your life that you'd rather not give them.

ACKNOWLEDGE OR REPLY TO EMAILS PROMPTLY

A professional responds quickly to emails. When I managed a staff, I made sure that if I received a message from any of my subordinates or consultants. I replied within a reasonable amount of time, usually within an hour or two, but certainly within the same day.

A recent boss demanded that all his employees reply to emails within four hours. This is a reasonable expectation for anybody on the payroll, yet that same manager virtually almost never even acknowledged receipt of an email. In fact, by actual statistic, he acknowledged one out of one hundred messages. I heard numerous complaints from customers and other employees. In fact, this was a major—if not the major—factor in my choice to move to a different job. It's difficult to work for someone who won't communicate an effective manner.

The same rule applies regardless of how the message is delivered. When I receive an inquiry on LinkedIn, I reply as soon as I'm able. If I receive an email message, I respond relatively quickly. I return phone calls as soon as I'm able.

For me, this is part of being a professional.

At another company, we had a severe system failure. The central computer was down for three days. This was a major disaster and affected the entire company. I was the poor soul, along with a couple of consultants and employees, who handled recovering from this failure.

I spent several hours putting together a long, detailed message to a senior manager to ensure that he understood that the root causes of the problem were understood and addressed. I agonized over the message because it was important to me that he have the information.

I never received a response. This was highly unprofessional behavior on his part. Regardless of what he thought of the

Email and Texting

information, a simple reply with, "Thank you for the information," would've been fine and appreciated.

By not replying, he communicated that he didn't care. It was very disheartening, and even worse, not responding or acknowledging was his modus operandi.

When a professional receives an email message from someone in the organization or someone attached to the organization such as a consultant, he or she responds in a reasonable amount of time.

USE CC WISELY

I've known many people who love to use the CC (carbon copy) function of email on a regular and constant basis. One man I worked with always CC'd a dozen or more people each and every time he sent out a message.

Professionals don't do that; instead, they send messages to particular individuals who have a need to be involved in the communication.

An email message (excluding broadcasts and newsletters which go to many people) should be addressed to one, or a small number, of recipients. The person or people listed under TO are the people to whom the email is intended to be delivered.

Include in the CC people who need to see the message but who do not need to take any action based upon the message. For example, if you're going to send an email to your consultants approving a contract, you might include your boss in the CC so he's aware of it happening.

In general, those who include large numbers of recipients in the CC field are trying to "cover their ass." By doing this, they needlessly involve individuals who gain no value from the information. This wastes the time of those people.

Thus, before you add a person to the CC of an email, ask yourself if they really need the information. If they don't, then don't add them.

DON'T USE REPLY ALL

When you hit the REPLY ALL command for an email message, you are sending the reply to everybody addressed in the message, including everyone listed under the CC.

In some jobs, it is quite common for people to respond to messages with, "Thank you," "You're welcome," and other mindless platitudes. It's fine to thank people; it's another thing entirely to send a thank you to the fifty people who received the message.

Sometimes I've seen this become an absolute comedy. An email will go out to eight individuals, with an additional 40 people included in the CC. Often, the message wasn't all that important in the first place and could've just gone the one or two people. The first message would be followed by a dozen "thank you" responses, then a dozen "Your welcome" responses, and then just to make it ever more fun, someone would reply with "Knock it off," which again went to everyone's inbox.

The answer is to use REPLY when replying unless you need the reply to go to everyone addressed in the message. Even then, take a look at the people in the CC and delete those who don't need to see the reply.

KEEP YOUR INBOX CLEAN

I've gotten into the habit of scanning through my email inbox each and every day and handling each message entirely. I review each one, quickly, and immediately reply, delete, and/or file it. This ensures that I'm caught up on all of my email communications at the start of each day.

Many people will leave an email unread in their inbox for days or even longer at a time. In the business world, this is generally unacceptable. Email is used to communicate information, orders, and requests, and quite often it can't wait until you "get around to it."

Get in the habit of scanning through your inbox every day and handling everything in it, and when you're done, your inbox should be empty.

USE TEXTING SPARINGLY

Do not use texting for business purposes. Email, Skype, or even the phone are better methods for professional communications.

Many people find the small keyboards on smartphones to be difficult to use when composing anything other than a very short message.

Text messages may not be seen right away because they're not as visible as email. Most people have email accounts attached to their smartphone, tablet, home computer, and laptop. Text messages generally only go to a single phone, and thus may be easily missed.

Summary

- ➢ Keep email messages short and to the point
- ➢ Don't overuse CC
- ➢ Send email messages only to those people who need the information
- ➢ Except under rare circumstances, do not use REPLY ALL
- ➢ Assume that any email may be read by human resources at any time
- ➢ Do not use company equipment, phones and email accounts for personal use
- ➢ Use humor sparingly if at all in email messages
- ➢ Remember that emails do not communicate emotions
- ➢ Send out minutes as soon after the meeting as you can
- ➢ Acknowledge emails and reply as appropriate in a reasonable amount of time

Social Media

"Social media is changing the way we communicate and the way we are perceived, both positively and negatively. Every time you post a photo, or update your status, you are contributing to your own digital footprint and personal brand."
—Amy Jo Martin

The United States is a free country, with freedom of speech and freedom of expression, meaning you undoubtedly have the right to say what you want when and where you want to say it. In a perfect world, your Facebook® and other social media accounts would be inviolate and would not be visible to work unless you made it so.

In this world, however, Facebook, Google+®, AOL®, LinkedIn®, and your own blog are visible to work, potential employers, insurance agencies, apartment managers, and everyone else. What this means is that whatever you write can be seen by other people, and not necessarily only those you specify.

It is important to remember that regardless of privacy settings and security, it is trivial for data to leak from your social media account.

Additionally, there can be bugs, hacks, or settings that cause your information to get out into the open world. Also, anything you post can be forwarded or shared with others, which will get around any security that you set.

Social Media

In other words, if you put up those wild party pictures, and even if you set the security setting so that only friends can see them, your friends can still download and forward them if they desire.

Even services such as Snapchat can have security issues that cause photos that are supposed to have been deleted in seconds to wind up all over the Internet.

It is quite common for disgruntled employees to post grumbling messages about their boss, coworkers, and workplace at various sites on the Internet. Today, robotic software that scans the Internet looking for certain keywords and phrases exists. Companies can purchase access to this software and find out who has been saying what about them.

This means those scandalous comments that are posted on any site can be retrieved by anyone who wants that information.

Your wisest course of action is never to post anything online that you wouldn't want your mother, best friend, spouse, or boss to find out.

You can count on any potential employer doing a scan on the Internet for anything derogatory that you might've posted, and for any information about you.

It's also quite common for apartment managers, financiers, potential business partners, significant others, and anyone else to search the Internet to find out about you. All of this information can be found out easily, quickly, and completely legally.

You have the power to control the message that all of these people and organizations receive about you. Naturally, the influence that you have over what other people post is limited, but you can fine-tune the message that you put out there for all to see.

For business, start with your LinkedIn profile. Create an account, if you don't already have one, and fill in the profile accurately and completely. Under no circumstances put out a blank or very skimpy profile; that gives an appearance of unprofessionalism.

By putting up an accurate and informative LinkedIn profile, you define yourself to other businesses all over the world. Using a quick search, you can be found, and the information that you've written will be communicated. Check out the book Focus on LinkedIn for more details, or you can use a service such as LinkedIn Makeover to help you create an incredible profile.

Clean up your Facebook, Google+, AOL or whatever personal accounts you have. Tune the privacy settings to tune what you want to be shown to the outside world. Review every post that you've created, including those from other people and in which you are tagged, and delete anything unprofessional or that presents something other than the image of you that you want the outside world to see.

Create a blog about one or more subjects you are passionate and knowledgeable about. Update it on a regular basis, at least a couple of times a month. There are plenty of blog sites out there that make it trivial to create and maintain this online presence.

Go to your favorite search engine and look for yourself under your name and any nicknames. If you're like most people, you won't find very much, or you'll find a scattering of things that you've posted over a period of many years.

Review what comes up, and if you have control of it, decide whether to keep it, delete it, or modify it as you see fit.

By going through these actions, you can put out there into the world the information that you want others to know about yourself.

Make sure that you keep any derogatory comments about your office, company, workplace, co-workers, vendors, or consultants off the Internet.

This is because you can bet everything you post will be found at the worst possible time by the worst possible person, having the worst possible effect on your life.

If you have some control over negative information, take care of it and reduce the chances of that happening.

Summary

- ➢ Create and maintain an up-to-date and informative LinkedIn profile
- ➢ Rid your social media accounts of any information that you'd rather the world didn't know about you
- ➢ Create a blog and write about your passions

➢ Do not post derogatory comments about anything, anyone, or any company on the Internet.

Deadlines

"Deadlines refine the mind. They remove variables like exotic materials and processes that take too long. The closer the deadline, the more likely you'll start thinking waaay outside the box." —Adam Savage

Deadlines are vital to complete any job. Without targets with dates attached to them, tasks tend to go on and on and are often never finished.

If you want to get something done, you need to set a point in the future at which it will be completed. You can think of it as a goalpost.

I'm a professional writer, and I usually have anywhere from a dozen to three or four dozen different jobs going on at the same time. That's the way of the world when you are a freelance writer; you take the work that you can get and schedule it in.

Each of those jobs has a date associated with it, which is when the assignment is to be completed. It doesn't matter whether the assignment is for pay, for my own amusement, or for my own professional advancement. There is always a completion date because that sets the expectation of myself and the client.

These dates are not just pulled out of the air willy-nilly. They are important and the intention is to meet or exceed them.

Deadlines

A professional sets target dates, known as deadlines, and works to achieve them.

When I was an IT director and managed a large computer department, there were times I would have well over 100 projects going at the same time. For the most part, my projects completed as scheduled. Sometimes, dates changed—this was usually because of unforeseen circumstances such as illnesses, changes in scope, or adjustments to priorities.

Just because a date has been put out there doesn't give a manager leeway to force his staff to work additional time to meet those targets. One of the jobs of a leader and a manager is to be able to allocate resources effectively so as to meet the objectives that have been set.

If the target is important to the organization, then the organization must be willing to fund meeting the goal. To force employees to work – especially unpaid overtime as in the case of salaried staff – is unethical behavior. Requiring unpaid overtime from employees is one of the best ways to destroy engagement, demotivate staff, and chase away quality people.

Of course, there are exceptions, such as during an emergency. In a disaster, all team members are expected to pitch in as much as necessary to help. Those who refuse, without good reason, are not team members and that condition needs to be corrected or they should to be asked to leave.

Setting deadlines creates targets for employees and team members; without such targets, no one knows when the task is complete. Without dates, it is very difficult to set priorities, and tasks tend to be prioritized all as equally urgent.

Setting deadlines for tasks and projects helps people with their priorities. When you create a completion date, you implicitly establish a priority for that task or project.

To create the deadline for a project, you need to create deadlines for each of the subprojects and subtasks that are necessary to complete the project. All subordinate tasks and projects must have dates assigned to them before the deadline of the project can be determined.

There are plenty of books, courses, and even certification programs on how to run projects and set deadlines. My point here is that professionals set deadlines for tasks and projects, use those to determine priorities, assign appropriate resources, and strive to meet those completion dates when possible.

Summary

- Create deadlines for all tasks and projects
- Without completion dates, tasks tend never to get done
- Deadlines must be achievable with the resources available
- Do not abuse employees to meet deadlines
- If the project is important to the company, the company must be willing to fund it properly

Integrity

"Corruption is worse than prostitution. The latter might endanger the morals of an individual, the former invariably endangers the morals of the entire country." —Karl Kraus

Quite possibly the most important characteristic of a professional is integrity. Integrity is defined as, "adherence to moral and ethical principles; soundness of moral character; honesty" (dictionary.com).

One measure of a person's integrity is how well they keep their word once given. If a person makes a promise and doesn't keep it, without good reason, then that person is showing a lack of integrity. This applies both to the workplace and for life in general.

You could think of a deadline as a promise to complete a task or project by a given date. Thus, a consistent failure to meet goals and targets would indicate a lack of integrity. Conversely, a professional with integrity will generally complete tasks on time.

Another measure of integrity is adherence not just to the letter of the law but to its spirit as well. A criminal is a person who has lost their integrity. On the other hand, a person with integrity understands what a rule, procedure or law is trying to achieve and goes the extra mile to adhere to that understanding.

When you hire someone for a position, it is understood that that person meets the qualifications for the job. Of course,

Integrity

there are going to be gaps in knowledge and experience, but still, it is expected that the person is willing fill those gaps and do the job to the best of their abilities.

Many years ago, I hired a programmer to work on an application for our company. This young man claimed that he was an expert and had extensive experience in that area. Work on the application didn't go well, and upon investigation I determined that he actually had no experience with that programming language at all. When he was confronted, he admitted that he lied on his resume and in interviews because he needed the job and felt he had to lie to get it.

This showed a lack of integrity on the part of that person. Needless to say, he was fired with cause. These lies and incompetence led directly to the failure of the application to make it to market.

I had a manager many years ago who was mildly abusive to his subordinates. We all used to dread our "walks around the block" where we would be berated at length for the smallest issue or concern.

Fits of anger such as that are counterproductive and lead to loss of productivity. It is better to manage with compassion and understanding than to try and control with lower emotions such as terror, fear, anger, and hate.

A person with integrity understands that abusive behavior is not appropriate under any conditions in the workplace. Emotions such as anger are never suitable for the job environment and are inexcusable on the part of a manager.

Integrity breeds respect. If you are honest, live up to your own standard of ethics, and treat others with honor, then you will be granted respect.

For a manager to be optimally effective, she needs to be respected by her subordinates, her peers, and those above her on the organization chart. Fear does not take the place of respect. You can cause people to get the job done if they fear you, but their engagement will be lacking and they most likely will be looking for employment elsewhere.

When you have integrity and you live up to it, other people notice. Conversely, they also will see a lack of integrity, ethics, and morals.

People learn by example. If you are successful, people will look at you and follow your lead. By demonstrating integrity, you show other people how to live with honor and ethics, and thus you help them survive better.

Thus, a professional understands that others are watching him or her and will learn by example. This makes it vital that they live up to the highest possible standards at all times.

Summary

- ➢ Fulfill promises that you make
- ➢ Be compassionate to people around you
- ➢ If you have integrity you will be respected
- ➢ Follow the spirit as well as the letter of the law, the rules, and the procedures
- ➢ Set a good example for others

Separation Between Work and Life

"No one ever said on their deathbed 'I wish I'd spent more time at the office.'" —Harold Kushner

Think about the role of work in life. What is the purpose of work? Early in my career, for various reasons, work became my life. I worked 60 hours a week or more. I brought my work home with me so that I could do even more, and virtually every waking moment was taken up by contributing to my job.

It goes without saying that after a few years of following this routine, I became immensely unhappy. Life seemed unfulfilling, and I grew very frustrated and angry.

Much later, I learned that there is life outside of work. It came as a shock to me, as weird as that might seem. It was as if I had woken from a nightmare and found there was something more to life than earning a paycheck.

This realization was a result of the horror of living through almost a decade of being a caregiver for my terminally ill wife. During those 10 years, my life split between work and her, and there wasn't room for much else. Because of the Internet, I was able to do much of my job from home. So I did my job and kept an eye on her.

When she died, I decided to get out into the world and attempt to handle the grief and pain of her loss. I visited botanical gardens and festivals, shows, and national parks, took rides in hot air balloons, and went on a cruise.

Separation Between Work and Life

I came back to life, and I realized that there was more to living than work. Of course, work remained important; after all, it paid the bills and funded things.

As a result of all this, I reoriented my life to get out into nature, be with family and friends, and pursue hobbies. It took a while, but the rewards were incredible.

I felt the life flowing back into me as I expanded outward from work into the world.

The lesson that I learned, and the lesson that I want to impart to you, my reader, is that work is important. For most of us, work is a vital part of life. But it is not everything, and it is not worth our integrity, all of our time, and all of our attention.

One of the hallmarks of a professional is understanding that there is a balance between work and life. A job is important, but it is not the most important thing in one's life. Most of us have to hold a job and do work on a regular basis, that is a part of life in this world.

It is important that when we get home, we put the cares of the office aside and do other things. This includes the family, the world around us, our religions, and volunteer work, among other things. In fact, even our hobbies are more important than work, because hobbies help keep us sane.

To be truly professional, you also must understand that this point applies not just to yourself but to all the people that work for you and with you. Respect the time of other people outside of work. In other words, barring emergency, home life takes precedence over work life.

This translates into the real world in many ways. A manager must ensure there is adequate staffing to get the appropriate jobs done in the appropriate timeframe. To attempt to meet schedules which cannot be met with the staffing at hand by forcing employees to work extra-long hours is unethical and inappropriate behavior. If the job that needs to be done is important to the company, the company should be willing to pay for the resources that need to get it done instead of taking advantage of its employees.

Summary

- ➢ Work is not all important
- ➢ Sanity is more important than any job
- ➢ Maintain a good work-life balance; work comes second
- ➢ Ensure everyone on your team has the opportunity for life outside of work
- ➢ If a job is important to a company, then the company needs to fund it and not demand sacrifices from its employees

Conclusion

Regardless of whether you are an employee, manager, or the CEO of a multi-billion dollar company, you should strive to be a professional. By that I mean you should behave with the utmost integrity and with a strong sense of honor.

Professionals respect other people in the organization and are respected themselves. They believe that everybody on the team adds value, regardless of their rank or position in the corporation, and may act accordingly.

Equally important is honesty and exhibiting the self-control to understand the workplace is a place of work and avoid mixing their personal life with their office life. In other words, professionals keep themselves under control in the workplace.

Professionals understand that they set an example for others around them. Sometimes it's simple things like acknowledging emails or respecting your teammates that make a difference. Occasionally, it's not so simple, such as meeting deadlines without the resources required to do so.

To become a professional, you need to decide to be a professional. As with any important goal in life, the first thing you have to do is make the decision to do it.

Thus, I challenge you to decide to be a professional, set a good example for others and to start on that road today.

Conclusion

Before you go

If you scroll to the last page in this eBook, you will have the opportunity to leave feedback and share the book with Before You Go. I'd be grateful if you turned to the last page and shared the book.

Also, if you have time, please leave a review. Positive reviews are incredibly useful. If you didn't like the book, please email me at rich@thewritingking.com and I'd be happy to get your input.

linkedin.thewritingking.com

About the Author

https://www.linkedin.com/in/richardlowejr
Feel free to send a connection request

Follow me on Twitter: @richardlowejr

Richard Lowe has leveraged more than 35 years of experience as a Senior Computer Manager and Designer at four companies into that of a bestselling author, blogger, ghostwriter, and public speaker. He has written hundreds of articles for blogs and ghostwritten more than a dozen books and has published manuscripts about computers, the Internet, surviving disasters, management, and human rights. He is currently working on a ten-volume science fiction series – the Peacekeeper Series – to be published at the rate of three volumes per year, beginning in 2016.

Richard started in the field of Information Technology, first as the Vice President of Consulting at Software Techniques, Inc. Because he craved action, after six years he moved on to work for two companies at the same time: he was the Vice President of Consulting at Beck Computer Systems and the Senior Designer at BIF Accutel. In January 1994, Richard found a home at Trader Joe's as the Director of Technical Services and Computer Operations. He remained with that incredible company for almost 20 years before taking an early retirement to begin a new life as a professional writer. He is currently the CEO of The Writing King, a company that provides all forms of writing services, the owner of The EBay King, and a Senior Branding Expert for LinkedIn Makeover. You can find a current list of all books on his Author Page and

About the Author

take a look at his exclusive line of coloring books at The Coloring King.

Richard has a quirky sense of humor and has found that life is full of joy and wonder. As he puts it, "This little ball of rock, mud, and water we call Earth is an incredible place, with many secrets to discover. Beings fill our corner of the universe, and some are happy, and others are sad, but each has their unique story to tell."

His philosophy is to take life with a light heart, and he approaches each day as a new source of happiness. Evil is ignored, discarded, or defeated; good is helped, enriched, and fulfilled. One of his primary interests is to educate people about their human rights and assist them to learn how to be happy in life.

Richard spent many happy days hiking in national parks, crawling over boulders, and peering at Indian pictographs. He toured the Channel Islands off Santa Barbara and stared in fascination at wasps building their homes in Anza-Borrego. One of his joys is photography, and he has photographed more than 1,200 belly dancing events, as well as dozens of Renaissance fairs all over the country.

Because writing is his passion, Richard remains incredibly creative and prolific; each day he writes between 5,000 and 10,000 words, diligently using language to bring life to the world so that others may learn and be entertained.

Richard is the CEO of The Writing King, which specializes in fulfilling any writing need. You can find out more at https://www.thewritingking.com/, and emails are welcome at rich@thewritingking.com

Books by Richard G Lowe Jr.

Business Professional Series

On the Professional Code of Ethics and Business Conduct in the Workplace – Professional Ethics: 100 Tips to Improve Your Professional Life - have you ever wondered what it takes to be successful in the professional world? This book gives you some tips that will improve your job and your career.

Help! My Boss is Whacko! - How to Deal with a Hostile Work Environment - sometimes the problem is the boss. There are all kinds of managers, some competent, some incompetent, and others just plain whacked. This book will help you understand and handle those different types of managers.

Help! I've Lost My Job: Tips on What to do When You're Unexpectedly Unemployed – suddenly having to leave your job can be a harsh and emotional time in your life. Learn some of the things that you need to consider and handle if this happens to you.

Help! My Job Sucks Insider Tips on Making Your Job More Satisfying and Improving Your Career – sometimes conditions conspire to make the regular trek to a job feel like a trip through Dante's Inferno. Sometimes, these are out of our control, such as a malicious manager or incompetent colleague. On the other hand, we can take control of our lives and workplace and improve our situation. Get this book to learn what you can do when your job sucks.

Books by Richard G Lowe Jr.

How to Manage a Consulting Project: Make money, get your project done on time, and get referred again and again – I found that being a consultant is a great way to earn a living. Managing a consulting project can be a challenge. This book contains some tips to help you so you can deliver a better product or service to your customers.

How to be a Good Manager and Supervisor, and How to Delegate – Lessons Learned from the Trenches: Insider Secrets for Managers and Supervisors – I've been a manager for over thirty years I learned many things about how to get the job done and deliver quality service. The information in this book will help you manage your projects to a high level of quality.

Focus on LinkedIn – Learn how to create a LinkedIn profile and to network effectively using the #1 business social media site.

Home Computer Security Series

Safe Computing is Like Safe Sex: You have to practice it to avoid infection – Security expert and Computer Executive, Richard Lowe, presents the simple steps you can take to protect your computer, photos and information from evil doers and viruses. Using easy-to-understand examples and simple explanations, Lowe explains why hackers want your system, what they do with your information, and what you can do to keep them at bay. Lowe answers the question: how to you keep yourself say in the wild west of the internet.

Books by Richard G Lowe Jr.

Disaster Preparation and Survival Series

Real World Survival Tips and Survival Guide: Preparing for and Surviving Disasters with Survival Skills – CERT (Civilian Emergency Response Team) trained and Disaster Recovery Specialist, Richard Lowe, lays out how to make you, your family, and your friends ready for any disaster, large or small. Based upon specialized training, interviews with experts and personal experience, Lowe answers the big question: what is the secret to improving the odds of survival even after a big disaster?

Creating a Bug Out Bag to Save Your Life: What you need to pack for emergency evacuations - When you are ordered to evacuate—or leave of your free will—you probably won't have a lot of time to gather your belongings and the things you'll need. You may have just a few minutes to get out of your home. The best preparation for evacuation is to create what is called a bug out bag. These are also known as go-bags, as in, "grab it and go!"

Professional Freelance Writer Series

How to Operate a Freelance Writing Business, and How to be a Ghostwriter – Proven Tips and Tricks Every Author Needs to Know about Freelance Writing: Insider Secrets from a Professional Ghostwriter – This book explains how to be a ghostwriter, and gives tips on everything from finding customers to creating a statement of work to delivering your final product.

How to Write a Blog That Sells and How to Make Money From Blogging: Insider Secrets from a Professional Blogger:

Books by Richard G Lowe Jr.

Proven Tips and Tricks Every Blogger Needs to Know to Make Money – There is an art to writing an article that prompts the reader to make a decision to do something. That's the narrow focus of this book. You will learn how to create an article that gets a reader interested, entices them, informs them, and causes them to make a decision when they reach the end.

Other Books by Richard Lowe Jr

How to Be Friends with Women: How to Surround Yourself with Beautiful Women without Being Sleazy – I am a photographer and frequently find myself surrounded by some of the most beautiful women in the world. This book explains how men can attract women and keep them as friends, which can often lead to real, fulfilling relationships.

How to Throw Parties like a Professional: Tips to Help You Succeed with Putting on a Party Event – Many of us have put on parties, and I know it can be a daunting and confusing experience. In this book, I share what I learned from hosting small house parties to shows and events.

Additional Resources

Is your career important to you? Find out how to move your career in any direction you desire, improve your long-term livelihood, and be prepared for any eventuality. Visit the page below to sign up to receive valuable tips via email, and to get a free eBook about how to optimize your LinkedIn profile.

http://list.thewritingking.com/

I've written and published many books on a variety of subjects. They are all listed on the following page.

https://www.thewritingking.com/books/

On that site, I also publish articles about business, writing, and other subjects. You can visit by clicking the following link:

https://www.thewritingking.com

To find out more about me or my photography, you can visit these sites:

Personal website: https://www.richardlowe.com
Photography: http://www.richardlowejr.com
LinkedIn Profile: https://www.linkedin.com/in/richardlowejr
Twitter: https://twitter.com/richardlowejr

If you have any comments about this book, feel free to email me at rich@thewritingking.com

Premium Writing Services

Do you have a story that needs to be told? Have you been trying to write a book for ages but never can seem to find the time to get it done? Do you want to brand your business, but don't know how to get started?

The Writing King has the answer. We can help you with any of your writing needs.

Ghostwriting. We can write your book, which entails interviewing you to get your story, writing the book and then working with you to revise it until complete. To discuss your book, contact The Writing King today.

Website Copy. Many businesses include the text on their sites as an afterthought, and that can result in lost sales and leads. Hire The Writing King to review your site and recommend changes to the text which will help communicate your message and improve your sales.

Blogging. Build engagement with your customers by hiring us to write a weekly or semi-weekly article for your blog, LinkedIn or other social media. Contact The Writing King today to discuss your blogging needs.

LinkedIn. LinkedIn is of the most important vehicles for finding new business, and a professionally written profile works to pulling in those leads. Write or update your profile today.

Technical Writing. We have broad experience in the computer, warehousing and retail industries, and have

Premium Writing Services

written hundreds of technical documents. Contact The Writing King today to find out how we can help you with your technical writing project.

The Writing King has the skills and knowledge to help you with any of your writing needs. Call us today to discuss how we can help you.

www.ingramcontent.com/pod-product-compliance
Lightning Source LLC
Chambersburg PA
CBHW071510210326
41597CB00018B/2714